D1477498

RECORD

BY GEORGE KEENEN

Igneus Press

Bellingham, WA

Printed in the United States of America
First Edition
ISBN#978-1-891-272-12-7

All inquiries may be addressed to:
Igneus Press
3310 McAlpine Rd.
Bellingham, WA 98225

Book Design by Kelsey Parks

PREFACE

RECORD was first hand-printed with rubber stamps by George Keenen in San Francisco in 1976, then lost until 2018. (The photo shows it in its original form.) It soon fell into the hands of Sophia Kidd, who deemed it worthy of publication.

Keenen was in the van of rubber stamp artists in the '70s. He published the first of several stamp catalogs in 1976. Joni K. Miller & Lowry Thompson, in their comprehensive book about rubber stamps, *The Rubber Stamp Album* (Workman Publishing, N.Y., 1978), say that these early catalogs are "treasured by those who have hung onto them."

Actually, Keenen made four books, but only one has resurfaced. RECORD was 76 pages long and took two nights to write, with time off for coffee at Terminal Lunch in downtown San Francisco. In this book, lines of type separated by a double space represent the pages of the original.

Keenen is a former Poetry Editor of ART/LIFE Limited Edition Monthly. He lives on an island off the coast of Oakland.

January 2021

ALL RIGHT
I'LL DO IT
BUT WHAT
IS IT YOU
WANT ME TO
RECORD

I'M AFRAID
THAT IF
YOU WANT
SPECIFIC
ADVENTURES
I WILL HAVE
TO DISAPPOINT
YOU

IF ON THE
OTHER HAND
YOU WANT
NOTHING

I WILL
PROBABLY
TELL YOU

THE WHOLE
THING UP
TO NOW
I HAVE
NEVER
GAMBLED
I HAVE
NEVER

HAD
ANYTHING
TO
SAY
NOR HAVE
I EVER
AND THIS
MAY

SURPRISE
YOU
KNOWN
WHAT WAS
GOING TO
HAPPEN
IT WAS
NEVER

NECESSARY
I HAVE BEEN
AM
IN THE GRIP
OF
SOMETHING

I AM
COMPLETELY
HAD
THE FUTURE
COMES

AS A
FOREIGN
LANGUAGE
THE SUN
HAS OFTEN
BEEN AN
EMPTY
EYE

I WAS
GIVEN ONE
MISTAKE
QUESTIONING
MY
IMMORTALITY
I GREW OLD

I STILL
HOWEVER
DO NOT
KNOW
MY AGE
I CAN TELL
YOU THOUGH
PEOPLE
OFTEN

OFFER ME
THEIR
SEATS
I WAS
TAUGHT 2
ILLUSIONS
WHICH HAVE
HELPED

ONE WAS
THE
ILLUSION
OF BEING
IN MOTION
WHILE
STANDING

STILL
YOU CAN
PROBABLY
GUESS THE
OTHER

I HAVE
ON
OCCASION
BEEN
DESERTED
THAT
MAGIC
WENT

OUT OF
MY LIFE
AT THOSE
TIMES
HAVING NO
IDEA WHEN
THE MAGIC

MIGHT
RETURN
I
ABANDONED
MYSELF
TO A
CHARACTER
OF MY

OWN
DEVISING

ON
ONE
SUCH
CHANCE
I
CAME
TO
AMERICA

WHERE
PEOPLE
WOULD
RATHER
SEE ME ON
TELEVISION

HERE I
PUT
TOGETHER

A QUICK
FORTUNE
THEY CALL
IT A PILE
WHILE

AWAITING
WORD
WORD CAME
IT WAS
PERFECTION

PERFECTION
IS FOR
BEGINNERS
CAME FIRST
THEN CAME

ABANDON
PERFECTION
I DID NOT

STOP TO
DISMANTLE
THE FORTUNE

MACHINERY
BUT LEFT
AT ONCE
ABOARD A
GHOST
SHIP
ONE DAY
IN THE

GALLEY
THE CAPTAIN
HIMSELF
INSTRUCTED
THE CREW
THAT HE
WAS
QUOTE

MOLDING
THEM TO
THE
PERFECTION
OF HIS
SHIP
I WENT

OVERBOARD
AS I
ALWAYS DO
AND
DISCOVERED
THE
FOR LACK

OF A
BETTER
WORD
OCEAN

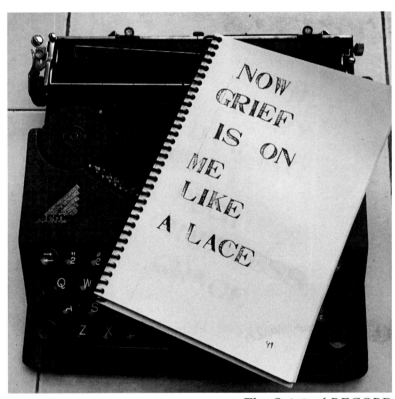

The Original RECORD

NO BREATH
UNDER
THE OCEAN
NO SIRENS
NO 2 THINGS
NO PLACE
OF YOUR OWN

WHEN SPRING
COMES
WHAT
QUICKENS
WHEN ALL IS
PULSE

ONE   NOTE
WHEN ALL
IS MUSIC
LAPS ON
SILENT
SHORES

PARTS OF
YOU
IN SO MANY
COUNTRIES
SPREAD
IF
LIKE A

TRAVELER
YOU REST
WHAT
COULD
NOT
BE
YOURS

IN ONE
GENEROUS
SEASON
YET WAVES
GO
UNDRUNK

THINGS
FLOAT
UP
UNGROWN
THE
SUN
MELTS

WHAT
YOU
ARE
LEFT
WITH
IS
ALL
THERE IS

I PUT THIS
IN
YOUR
BOOK
DEMAND
MORE

BUILD
CITIES
THAT
SINK
FOLLOW
THEM
DOWN

YOU
WILL
PERHAPS
PASS
BURIED
SONGS
RISING

IF YOUR
HEART
ACHES
LIKE
A JEWEL
TO
RISE

THEN
RISE
AND
RUST
FLIES
FROM
THE SUN

I
LEARNED
YOUR
VOICE
FROM
A COMMON
STAR

YOUR
SOUND
FROM
INSIDE
LIKE A
THIEF

TAKING
YOUR
WORDS FOR
JEWELS
THAT
SPROUT
FROM
THROATS

I
WORE
THAT
BLOODLIGHT
ON ME
LIKE A
SON

AND
SOMETIMES
KNEW
YOU AS A
DANCE

NOW
GRIEF
IS ON
ME
LIKE
A LACE

SUCH
SORRY
DANCING
SUCH
CHILDLESS
GRACE

DANCE
LIKE
THE
ORANGE
TREE
RETURNING

SUN
FOR
SUN
THIS CAME
TO ME

FROM
AN APPLE
I HAVE
LEARNED
TO LISTEN
WHICH IS

TO DANCE
WHICH IS
TO BLESS
THE WAY
DANCE
THE PRIEST

SWEET
COMMUNION
IF HE WILL
SHARE
HIS WIFE

DANCE
THE IRON HEEL
TO GRASS
DANCE
JUICE
TO BLOOD

LIE IN
THE
DANCE OF
SOMETHING
GREEN

AND
SLEEPING
YOU
WILL
CLIMB

TO HANG
LIKE
MAD
FEET
AWAITING
THE
RISING
EARTH

AWAITING
KISSES
ALL
ALONG
YOUR
TAPERING
LENGTH

WHERE
WORDS
LEAVE
OFF

WALKING
THE CITY
RESISTING
ATTRACTING

STALE
DANISH
INSIDE

OF THE
CITY
NOBODY
BUYS
ANYTHING

EVERYONE
IN DEBT
JACKHAMMERS
FOR A
WEEKEND
WITH A
BIG MOON

A MAN IN THE
CITY IS NO
MORE THAN
A RABBIT
IN A FIELD
OF
MECHANICAL
COWS

HIS
LARGEST
SHADOW
DIES AT
NIGHT
AND OTHERS
ARE
REBORN

WE WANT
WHAT
THE LAW
HAS
TAKEN
AWAY

EVIL
SHOWS A PROFIT
THAT MONEY
GOES FOR
GOOD WORKS

AND
GESTURES
WHILE
MILLIONS
DO A SLOW
ROT
ACROSS
FROM A

VACANT
LOT
WHICH
LAW
HAS GIVEN
TO THE
LIKES OF

BOISE
BAXTER
BOISE
WALKS
22 BLOCKS

ON A
COLD NIGHT

THEN
BACK
ALL BOISE
BAXTER'S PROBLEMS
TRAVEL

ACROSS
THE CITY
IN HIS
POORLY
TUNED
MACHINE
THERE ARE

MEN
WHO
WOULD
SURELY

KILL HIM
BUT HE
CANNOT
STAY
INDOORS

HAVE I
GOT
SOMETHING
FOR YOU
BOISE

IF
YOU'RE IN
THE GRIP
OF
SOMETHING

--FIN--

Igneus Press

Bellingham, WA